HEAD FIRST

BY MIKE DION
ILLUSTRATED BY BRADLEY CLARK

MODERN CURRICULUM PRESS
Pearson Learning Group

Cindy watched the kids on the swim team practice for the Girls' Diving Championship. Cindy didn't dive. She was sure she could—she'd just never tried. Her big brother knew how. He'd even won the Boys' Diving Trophy one year.

Laura Hale surfaced, shook her wet head, and laughed. Diving looked like fun. Cindy was a good swimmer, but she liked the sidestroke and the backstroke best. She hated to put her head underwater, and diving meant head first.

Diving had always been her brother's thing. Could she do it too?

Maybe she'd try diving now, while no one was looking. Cindy didn't want anyone to see what a wimp she was. So what if she got her head wet? She wouldn't melt!

She bent over and counted. When she got to *three* she sent herself into the water, head first.

Cindy came up choking, but alive. She coughed water out of her mouth. She was going to have to learn how to dive without swallowing half the pool.

She tried again, but this time she remembered to close her mouth before she went in.

"Want to learn to dive?" asked Ellen. She was the swimming instructor.

"Maybe," said Cindy. "What do I have to do?"

"Practice," said Ellen. "Besides practice, all you need is a coach and a good opponent."

Cindy saw why she needed a coach. She saw why she needed practice. But a good opponent? Why would she stress herself out by competing against girls who were already good divers?

"I don't need an opponent," she said. "I'm not going to dive in the meet."

"A good opponent will make you strive to do the best you can," said Ellen.

Cindy wasn't going to dive in the championship meet. But if she did, she knew who her opponents would be. Susan, Tracy, and Kelly were all good divers, and Laura Hale was better yet. Laura had won last year's championship trophy. Whoever won this year would have to beat Laura Hale.

Ellen showed Cindy how to point her arms with her head between them. She showed Cindy how to bend at the middle and at the knees. She made Cindy practice diving from the side of the pool, again and again.

Cindy thought five was a good number of practice dives. Ellen thought thirty was more like it. She made Cindy keep practicing until everyone else was out of the pool. Cindy practiced until her fingers turned blue. She wondered why Ellen made her work so hard when she wasn't even on the team.

Next Ellen took Cindy to the diving board and showed her how to use the spring in the board to help her dive. Cindy's first dive off the board was an ordeal. She didn't want to do it, but she couldn't back down either. She was scared, but also excited. It would be so great to be able to dive like Tracy or Laura! She was afraid, but she knew she was going to dive anyway.

In the next weeks Cindy practiced and practiced. She got used to going in head first and swimming underwater, but she couldn't seem to straighten out when she dived. Cindy bent like an elbow. She bent like a bow. She landed straight, but flat. That hurt! Good thing she wasn't planning to compete in the championship! It felt as if she'd never learn to dive like her best opponent, Laura Hale!

Cindy watched Laura dive. Laura sprang up from the board and bent like a hinge. She dove straight down like an arrow. Her legs stayed straight when she hit the water. Watching Laura dive made Cindy want to try again, and again, and again.

On the day of the diving meet, Cindy's family came to watch the competition. Cindy went to sit with them on the bench.

"It's good you're here!" said Ellen. "Come sit with the team!"

Cindy blinked. "What?"

Ellen gestured toward the team bench. Cindy went over and sat with the team.

"Susan can't make it," Ellen said. "You just volunteered to be number three!"

Number three for what? Suddenly Cindy didn't feel well. She watched Tracy dive, then Laura. Tracy's dive was good, and Laura's was excellent.

"Your turn," said Ellen.

"No way!" said Cindy.

Everyone was looking at her, and then her name came out of the loud speaker.

Cindy guessed she was competing in the championship diving meet after all. She tried to feel like a winner, but she only felt scared. *I'm a diver!* Cindy thought as she walked to the diving board. *I'm a champion!* she thought when she stood on the board. She wished no one were watching. She wished she were invisible. She wasn't just a little scared—she was championship-level scared!

Cindy couldn't wimp out of a championship meet. Her brother was out there and he could dive. Cindy took a deep breath. So she was scared! So what? Maybe she couldn't win, but she could do her best!

Cindy pointed her arms and sprang up from the diving board. She made herself into a hinge. She aimed her hands toward the water, and straightened her legs.

Cindy went into the water head first. She felt like a meteor, an arrow of light! She curved underwater. Diving was great! Now that she knew what a good dive felt like, she didn't even care if she won the championship! She just wanted to keep on diving.

Cindy shot out of the water.

"Good dive!" shouted Ellen.

Cindy grinned. Who would have thought she could hold her own in a diving championship? She knew she hadn't won any trophy. But she also knew she was a good opponent, and a pretty good diver.

Maybe she'd be even better by next year!